Color In Scripture

A Creative and Inspirational

Adult Coloring Book

Based On the Bible

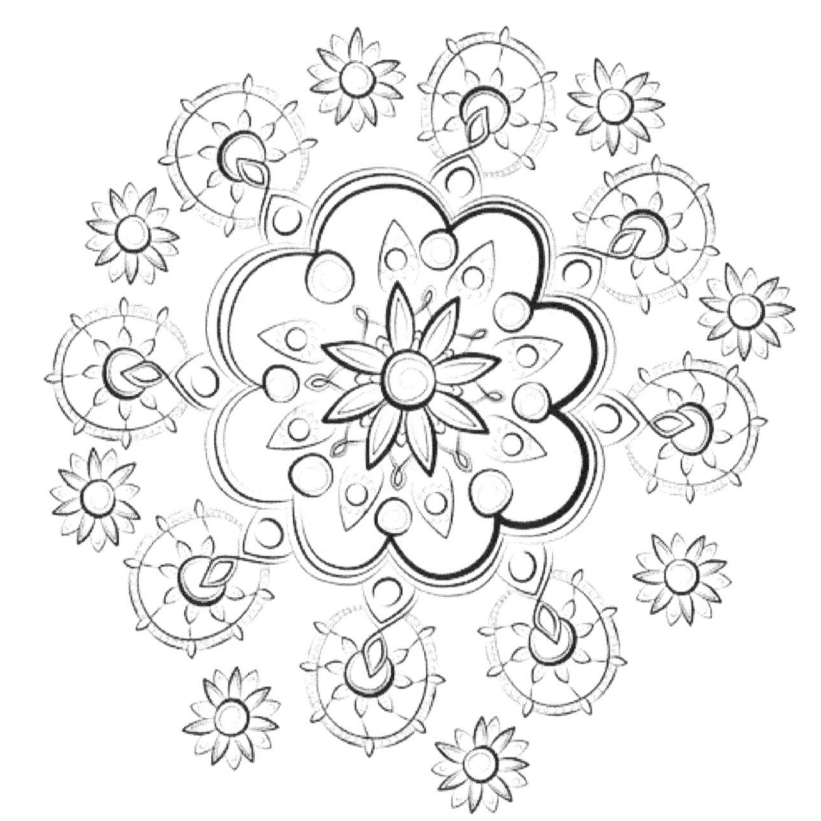

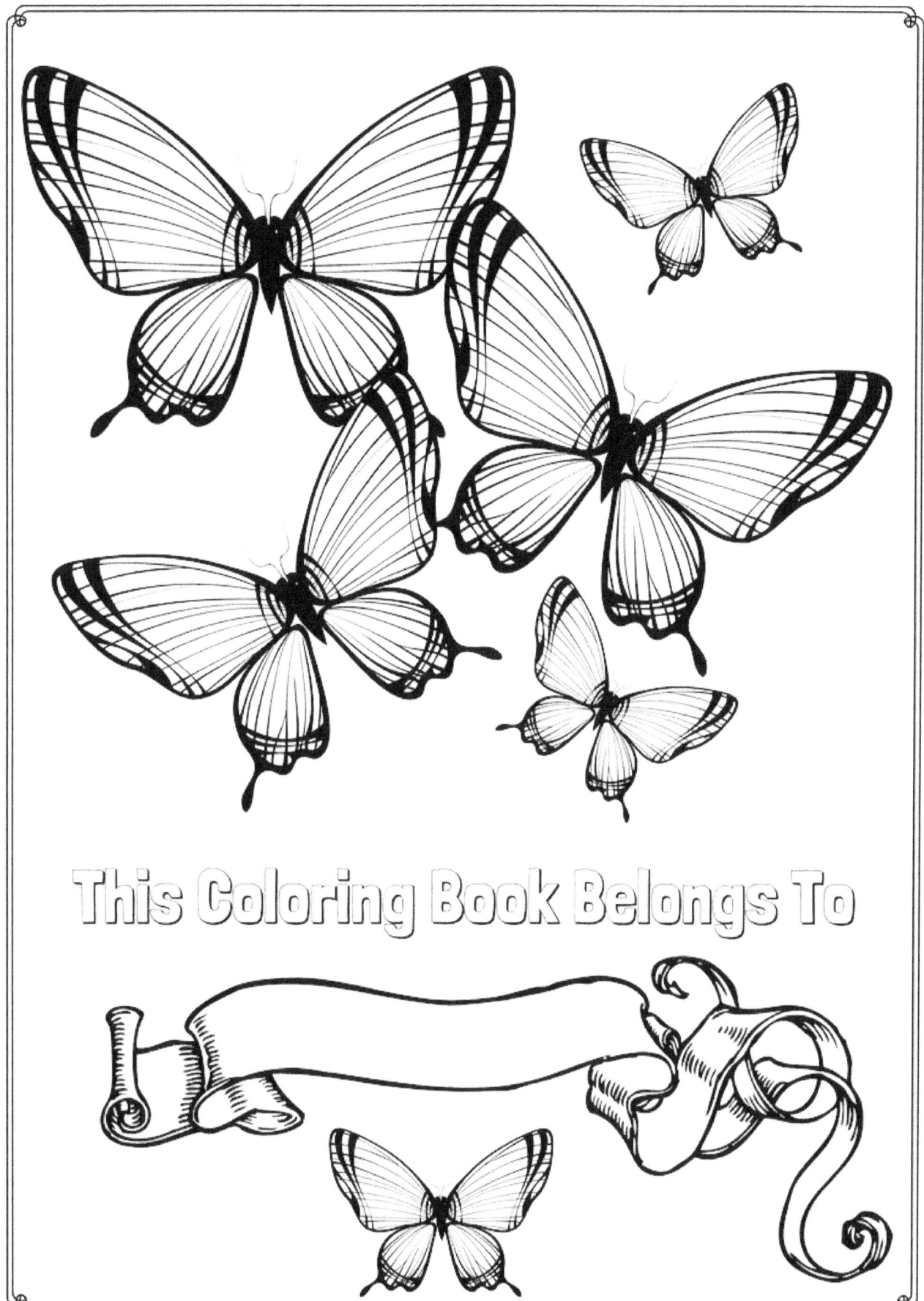

This Coloring Book Belongs To

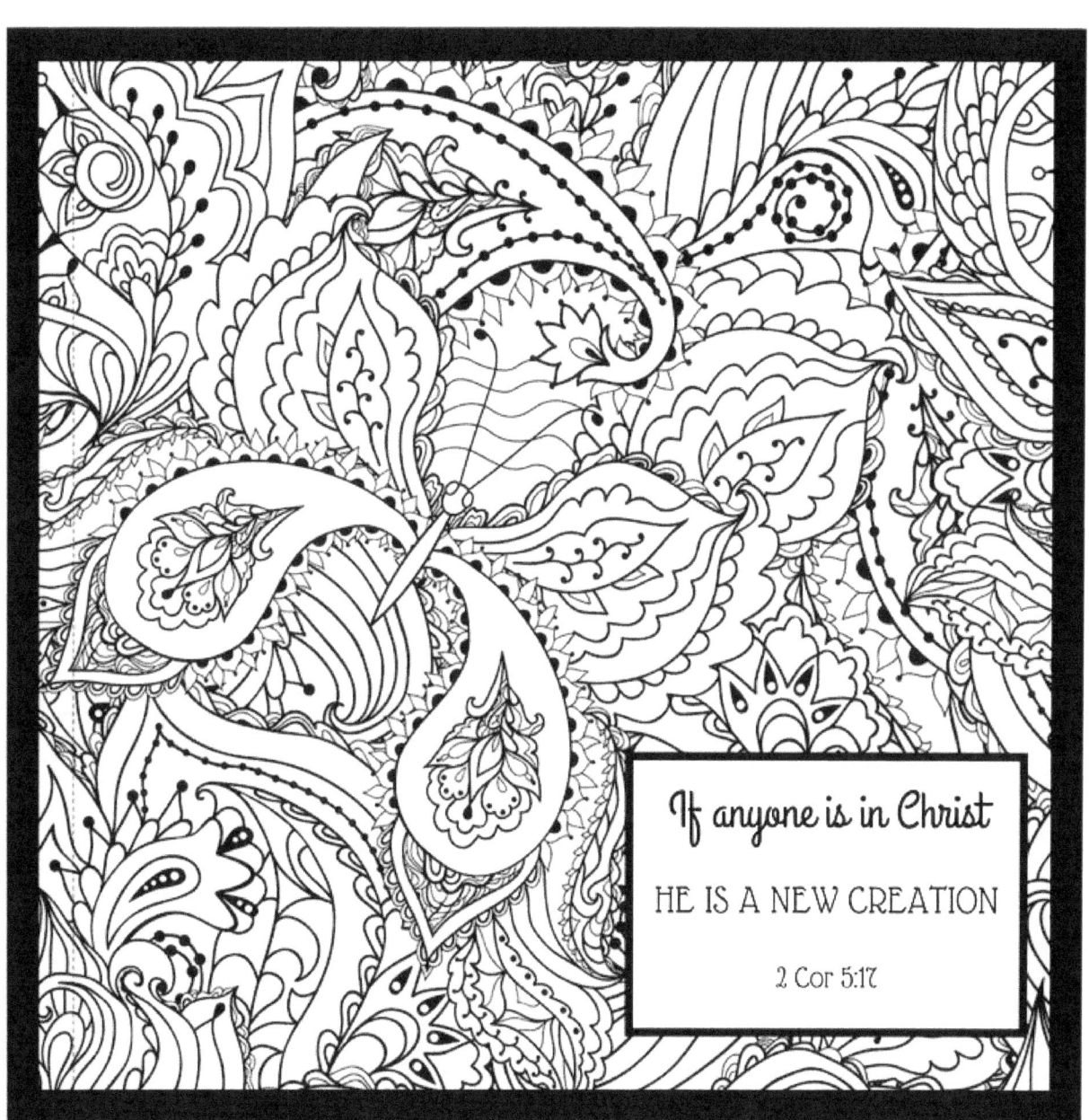

If anyone is in Christ

HE IS A NEW CREATION

2 Cor 5:17

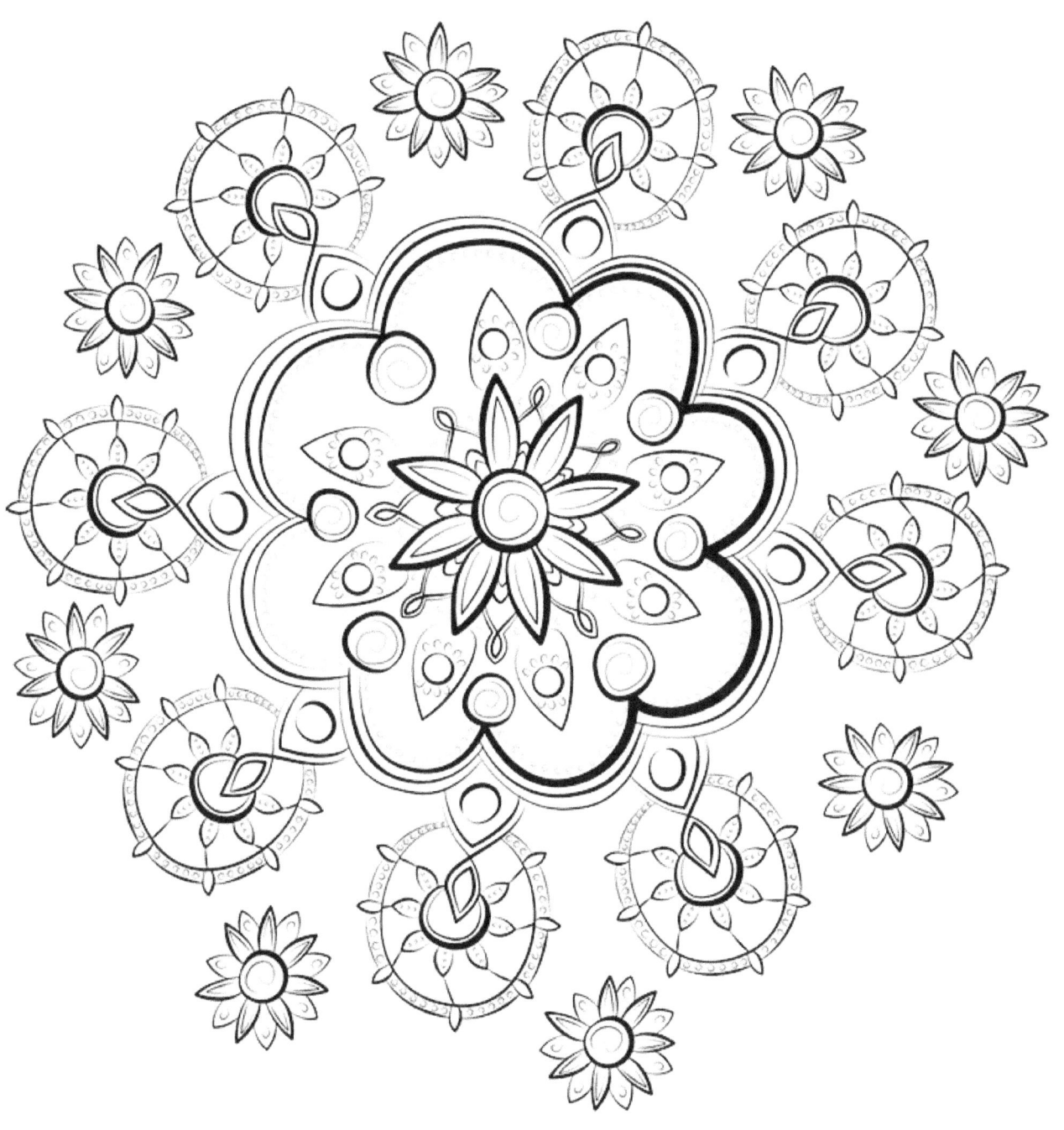

God didn't give us a spirit of fear,
but of power, love, and self-control.

2 Timothy 1:7

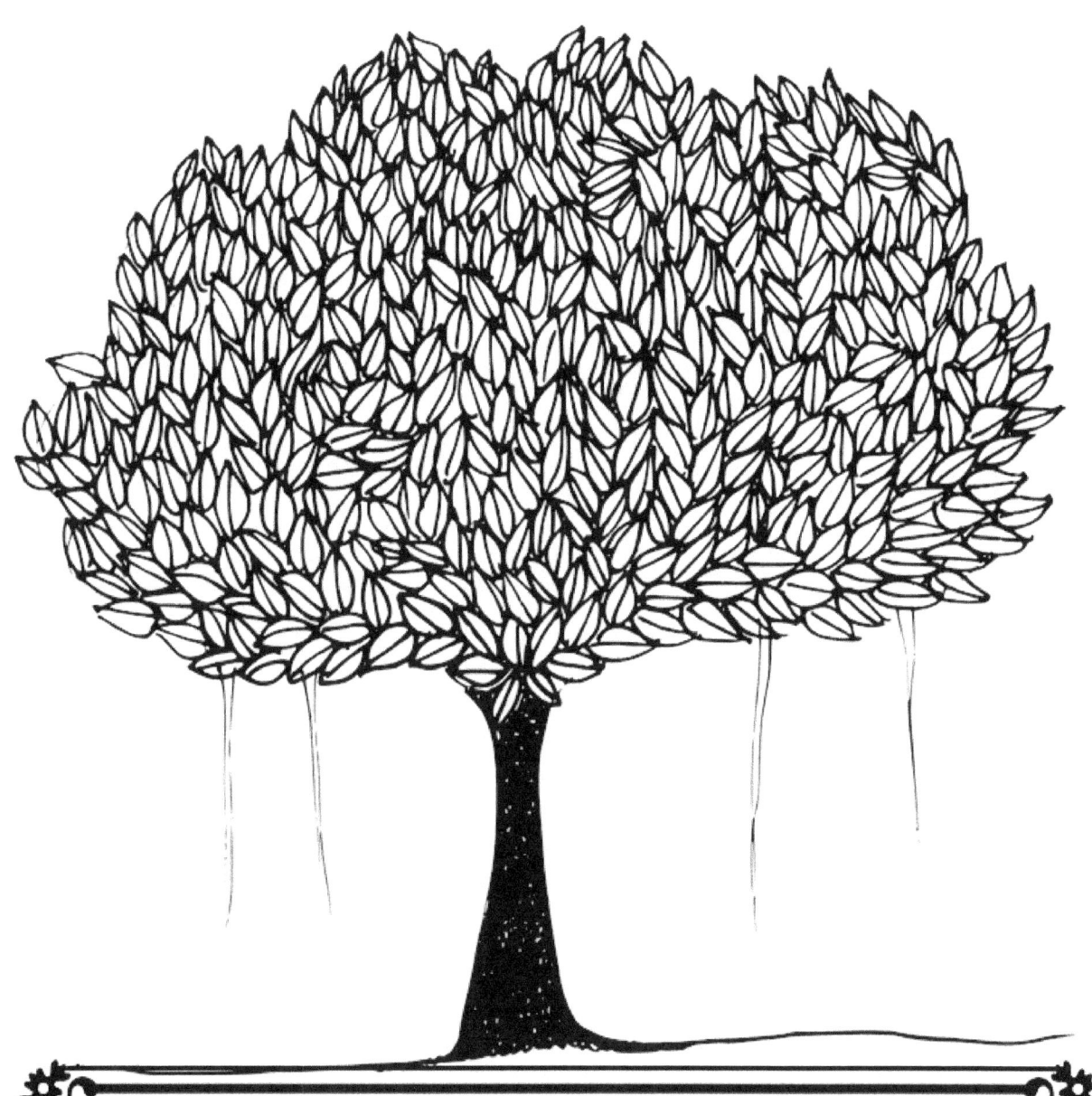

And he shall be like a tree planted by the rivers of water, that brings forth its fruit in its season; his leaf also shall not wither; and whatsoever he does shall prosper.

PSALM 1:3

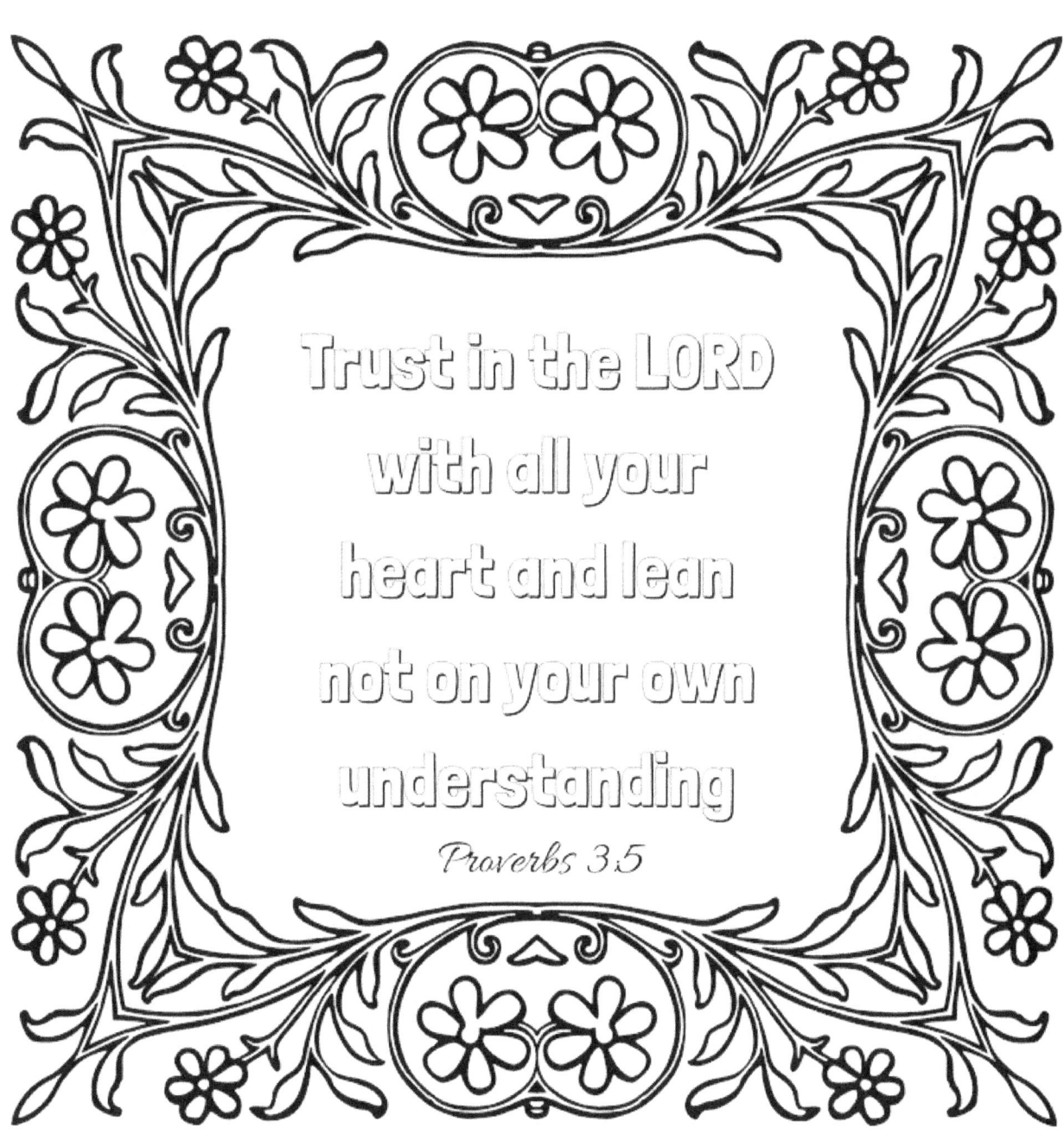

Trust in the LORD with all your heart and lean not on your own understanding

Proverbs 3:5

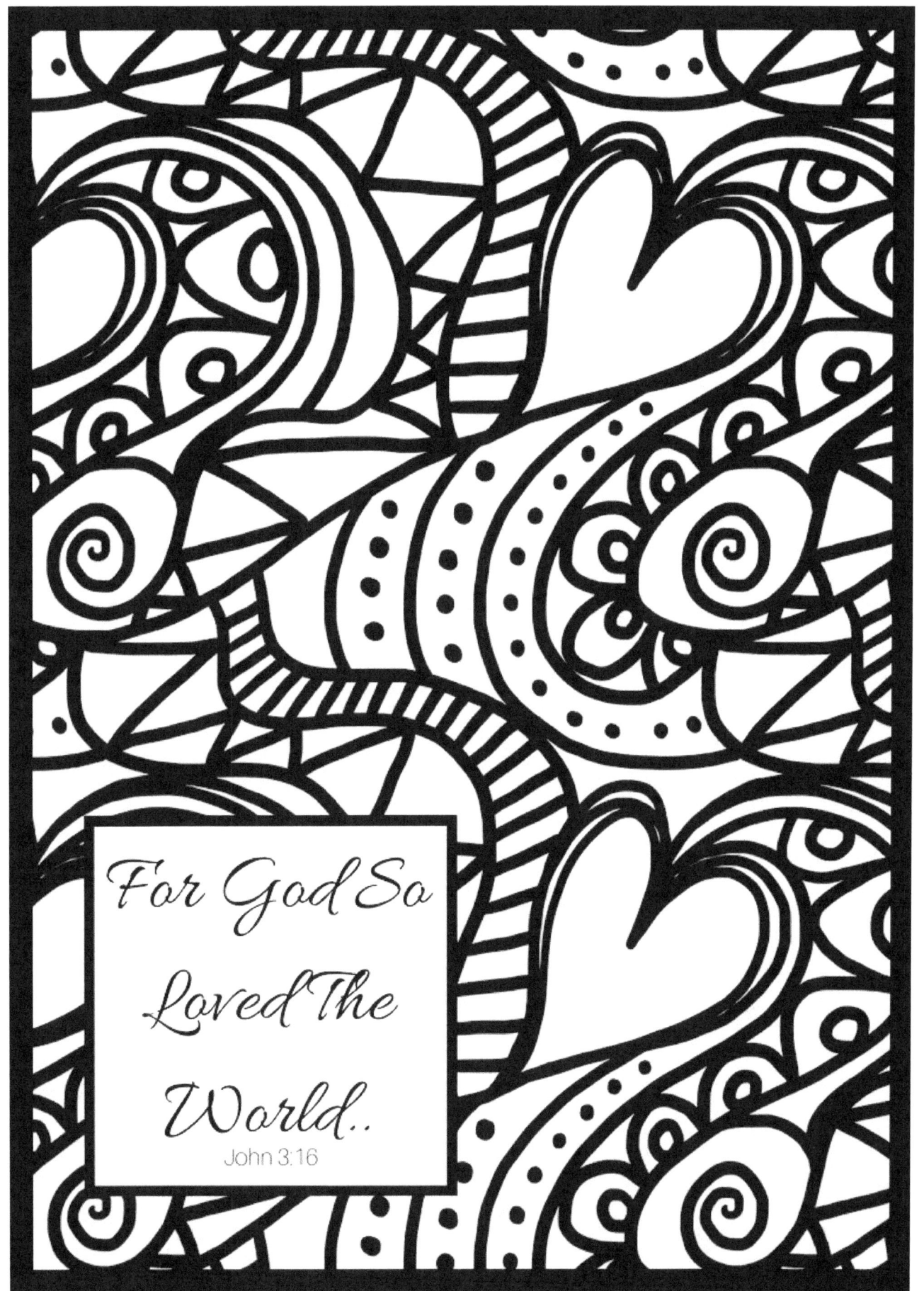

For God So Loved The World..

John 3:16

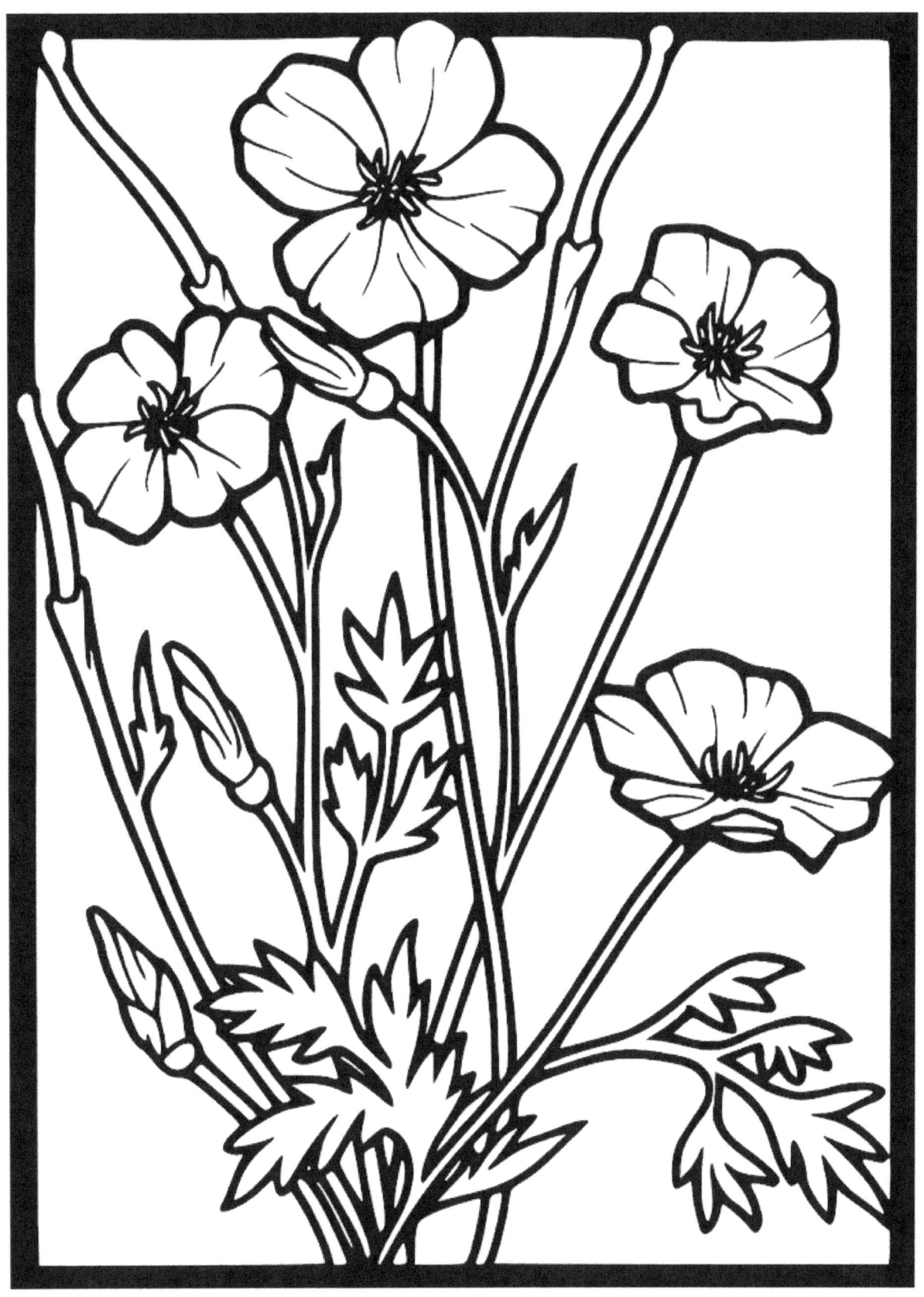

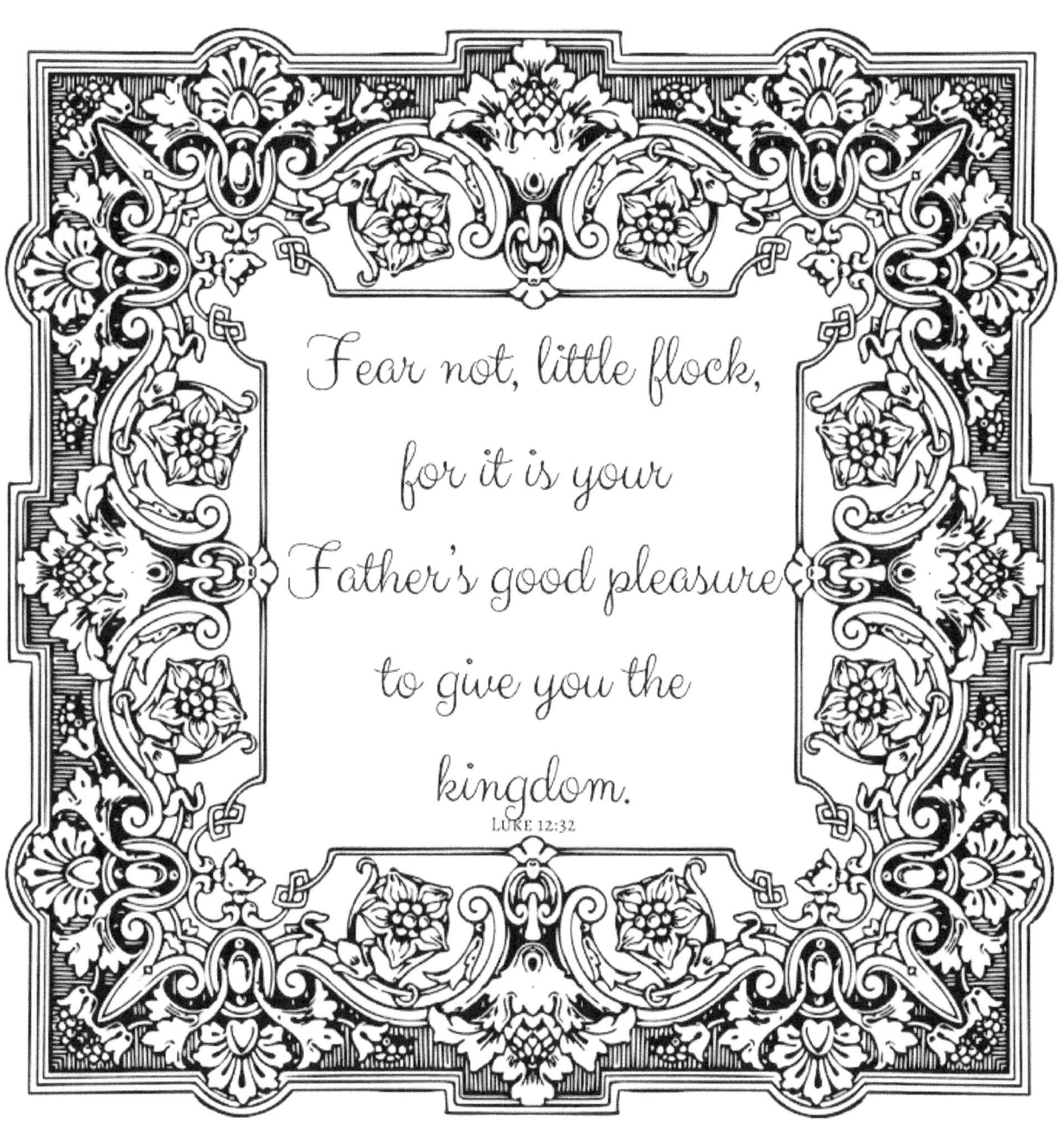

Fear not, little flock,

for it is your

Father's good pleasure

to give you the

kingdom.

LUKE 12:32

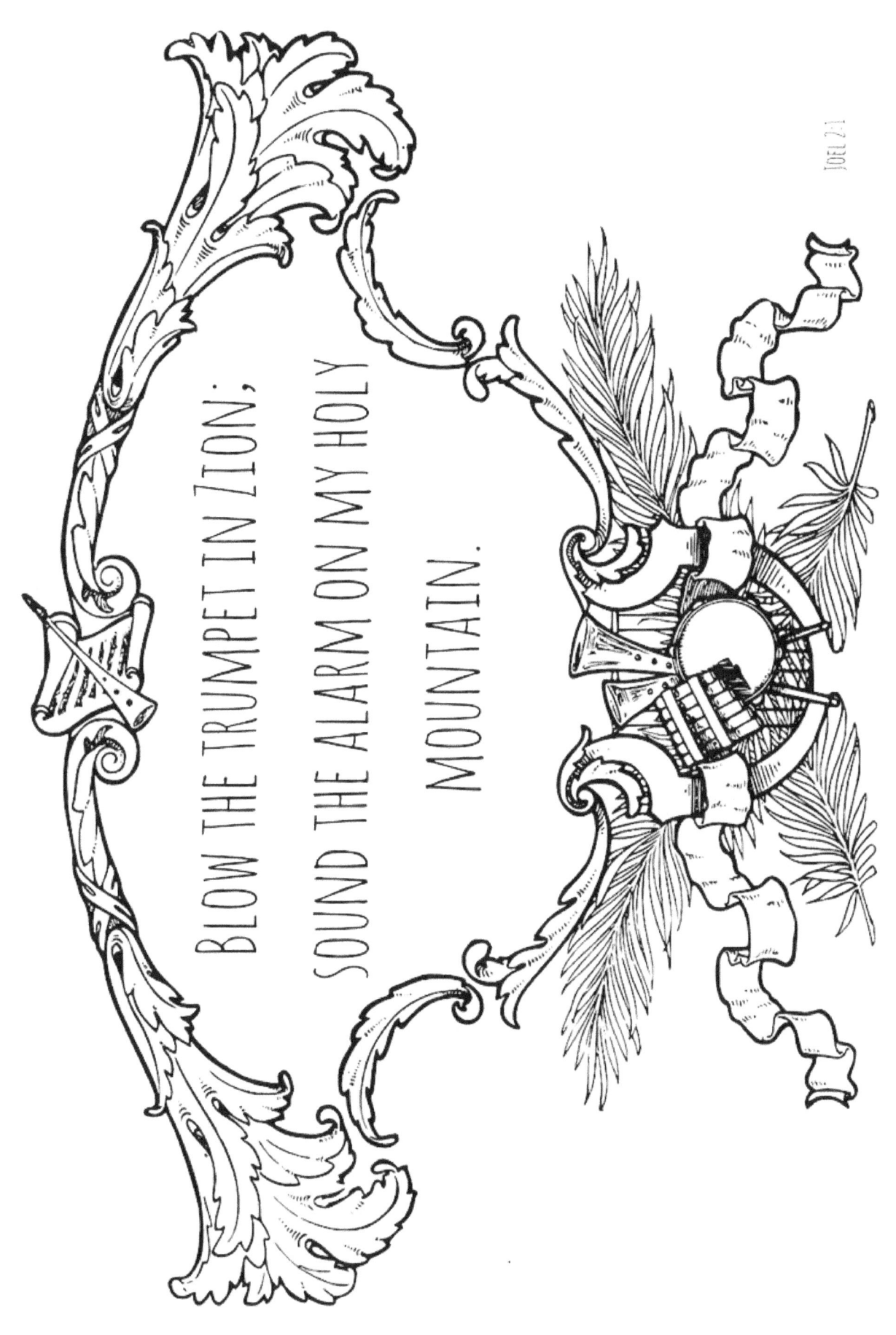

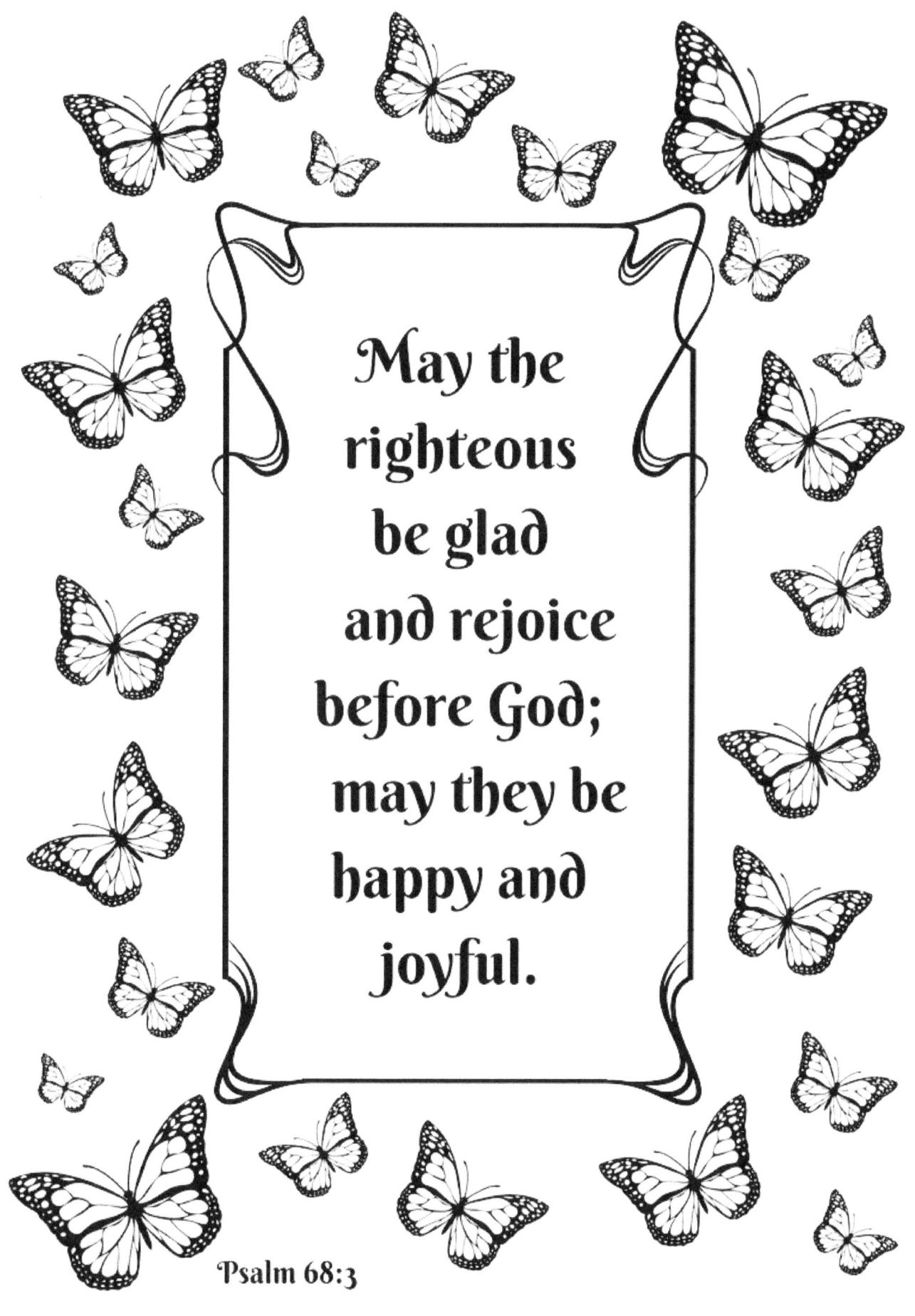

May the
righteous
be glad
and rejoice
before God;
may they be
happy and
joyful.

Psalm 68:3

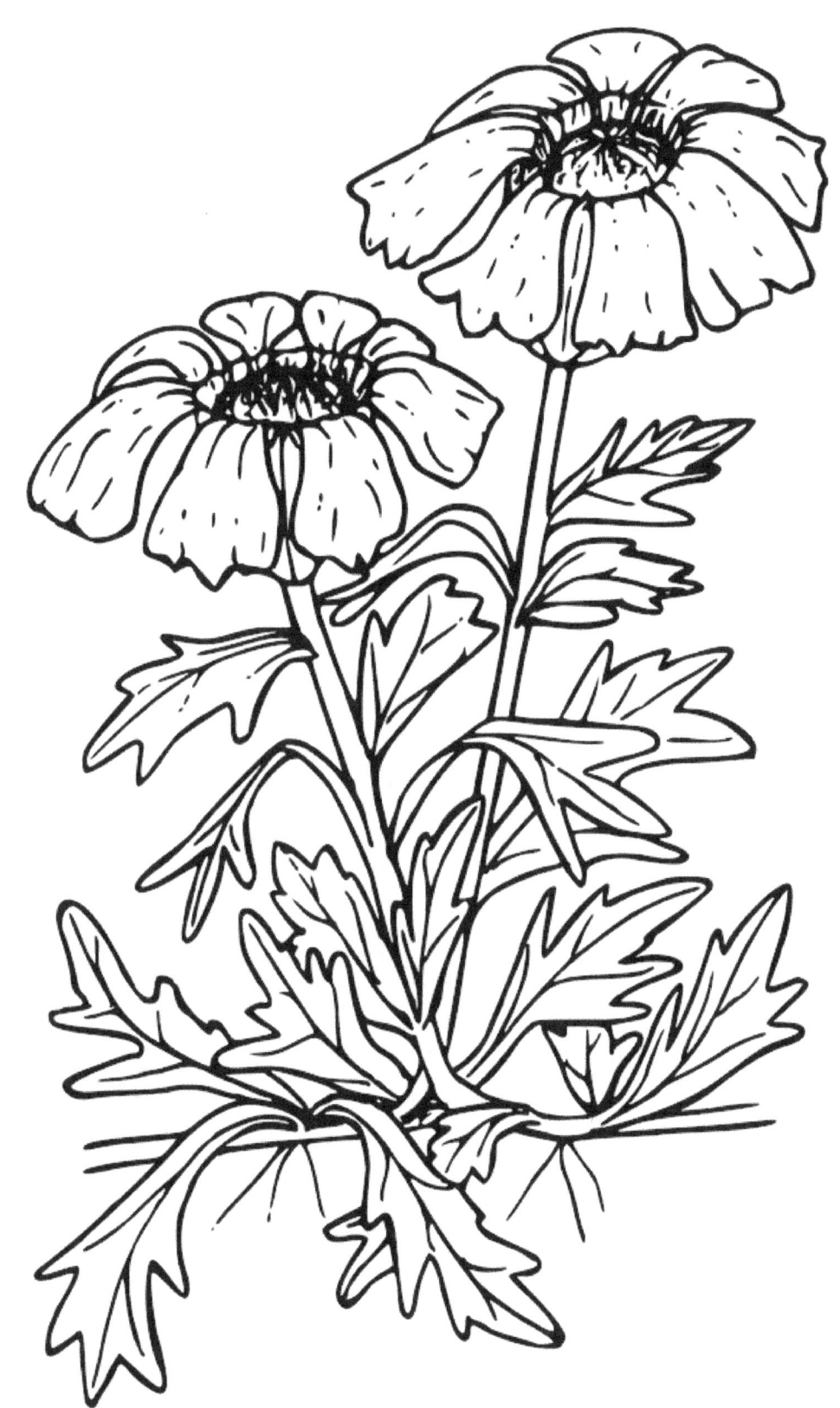

Speaking the truth in love, we will grow to become in every respect the mature body of him who is the head, that is, Christ. Ephesians 4:15

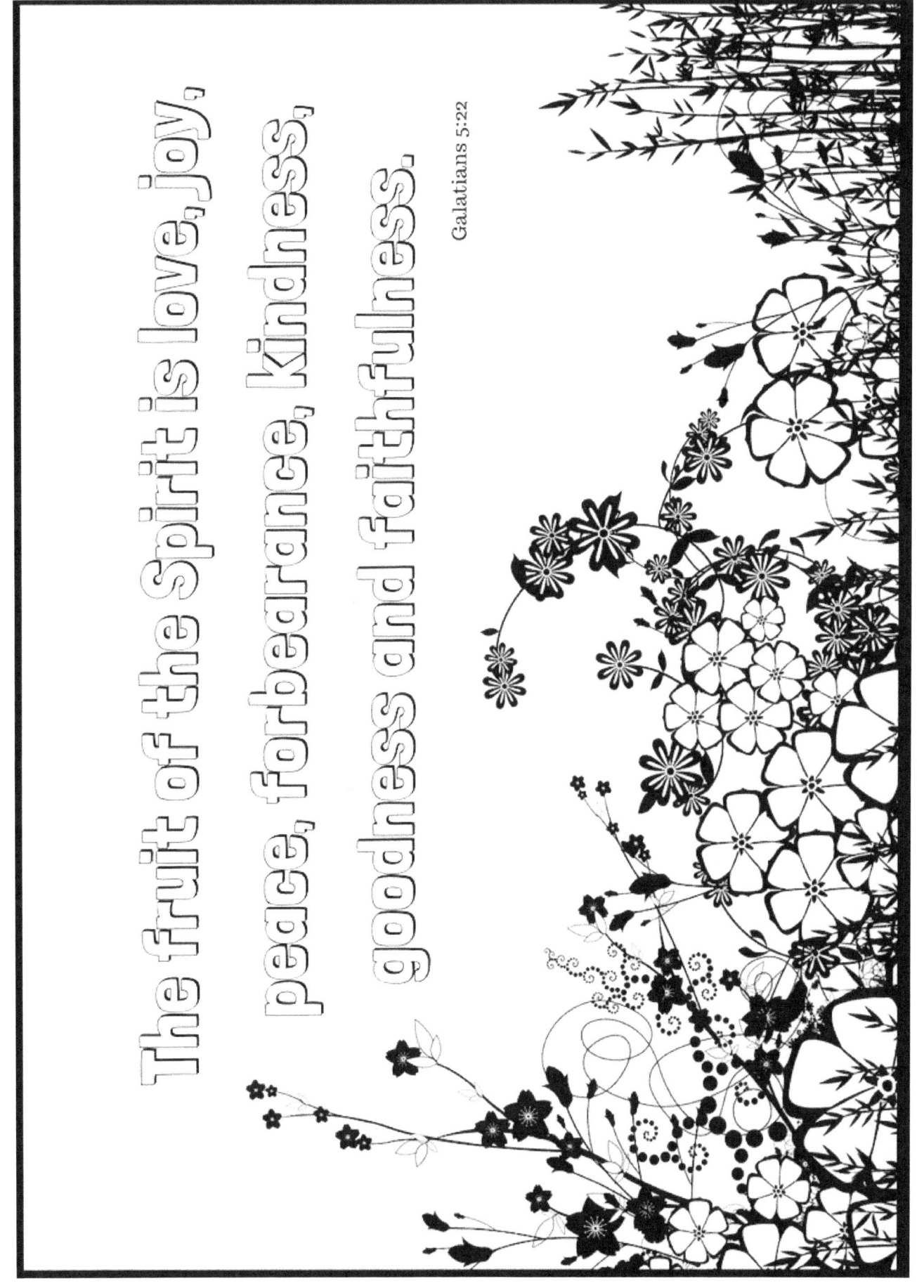

The fruit of the Spirit is love, joy, peace, forbearance, kindness, goodness and faithfulness.

Galatians 5:22

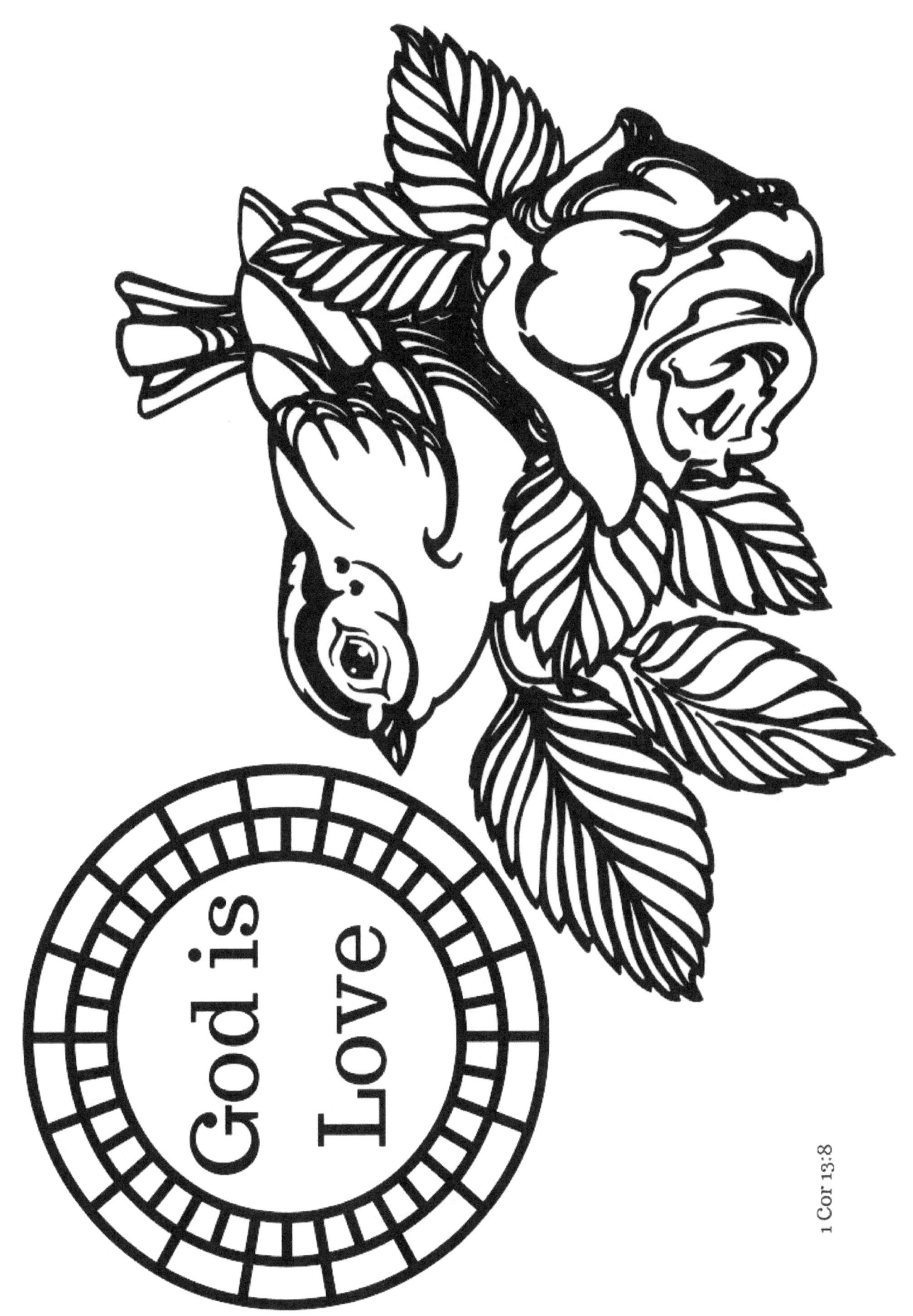

God is Love

1 Cor 13:8

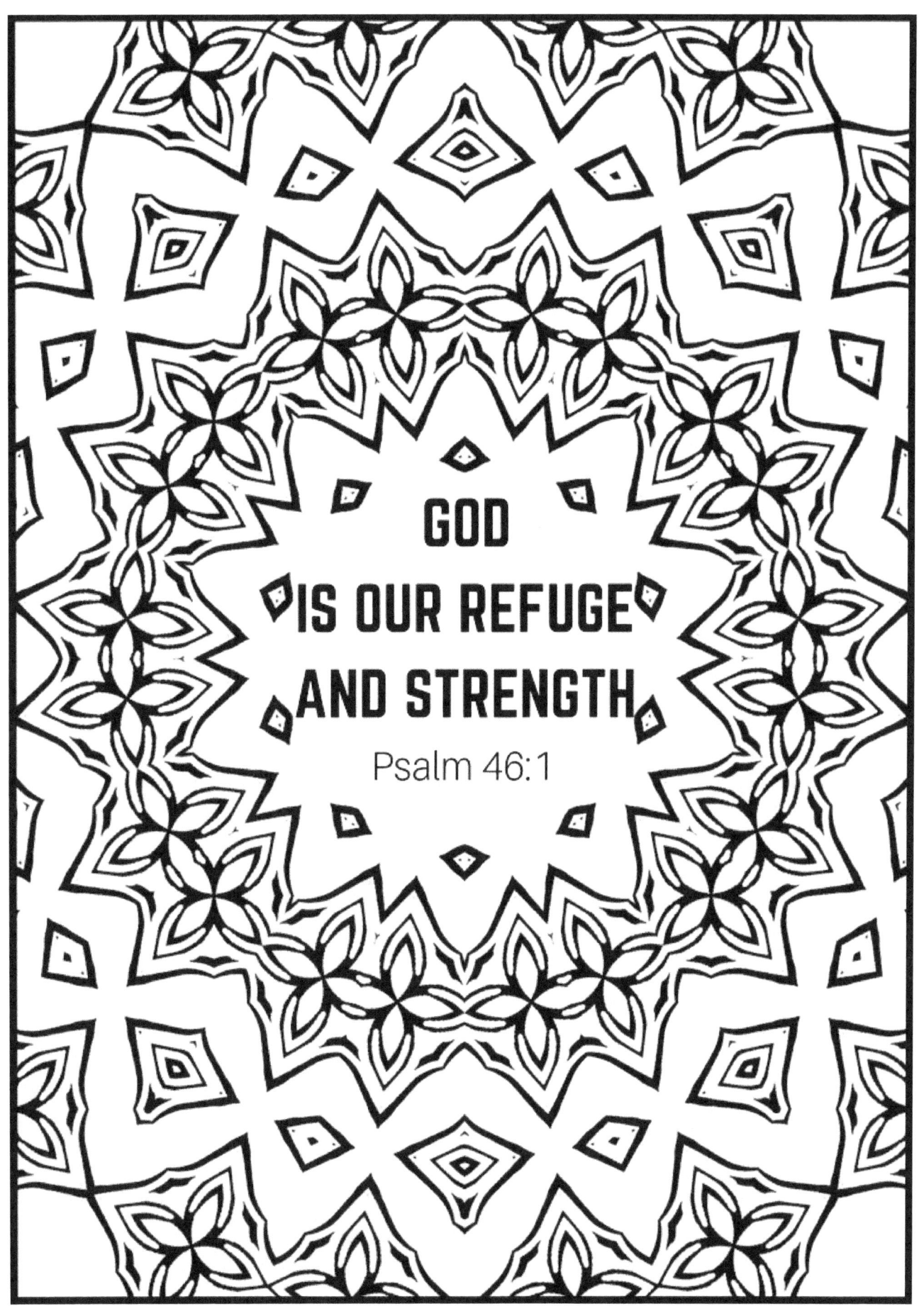

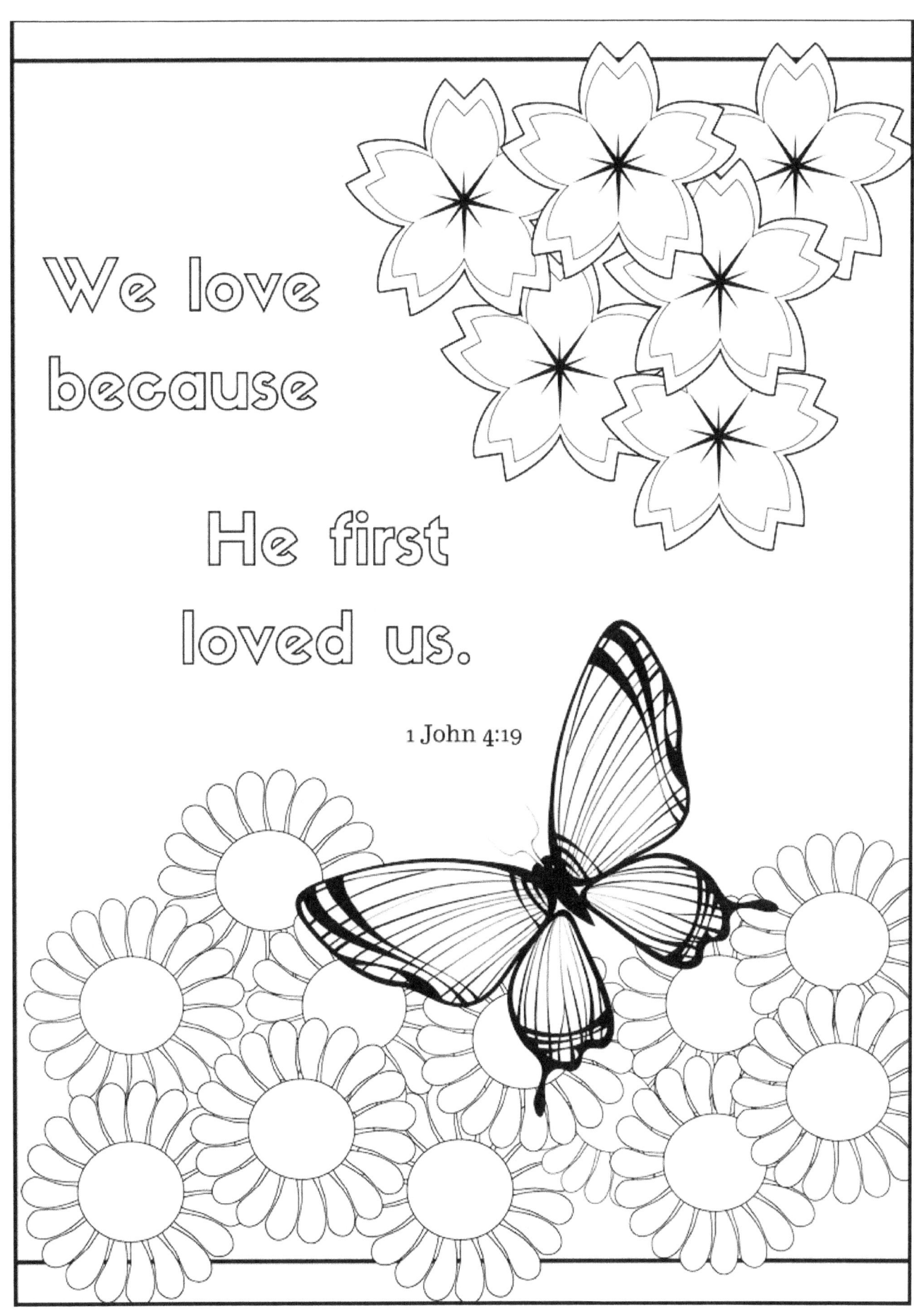

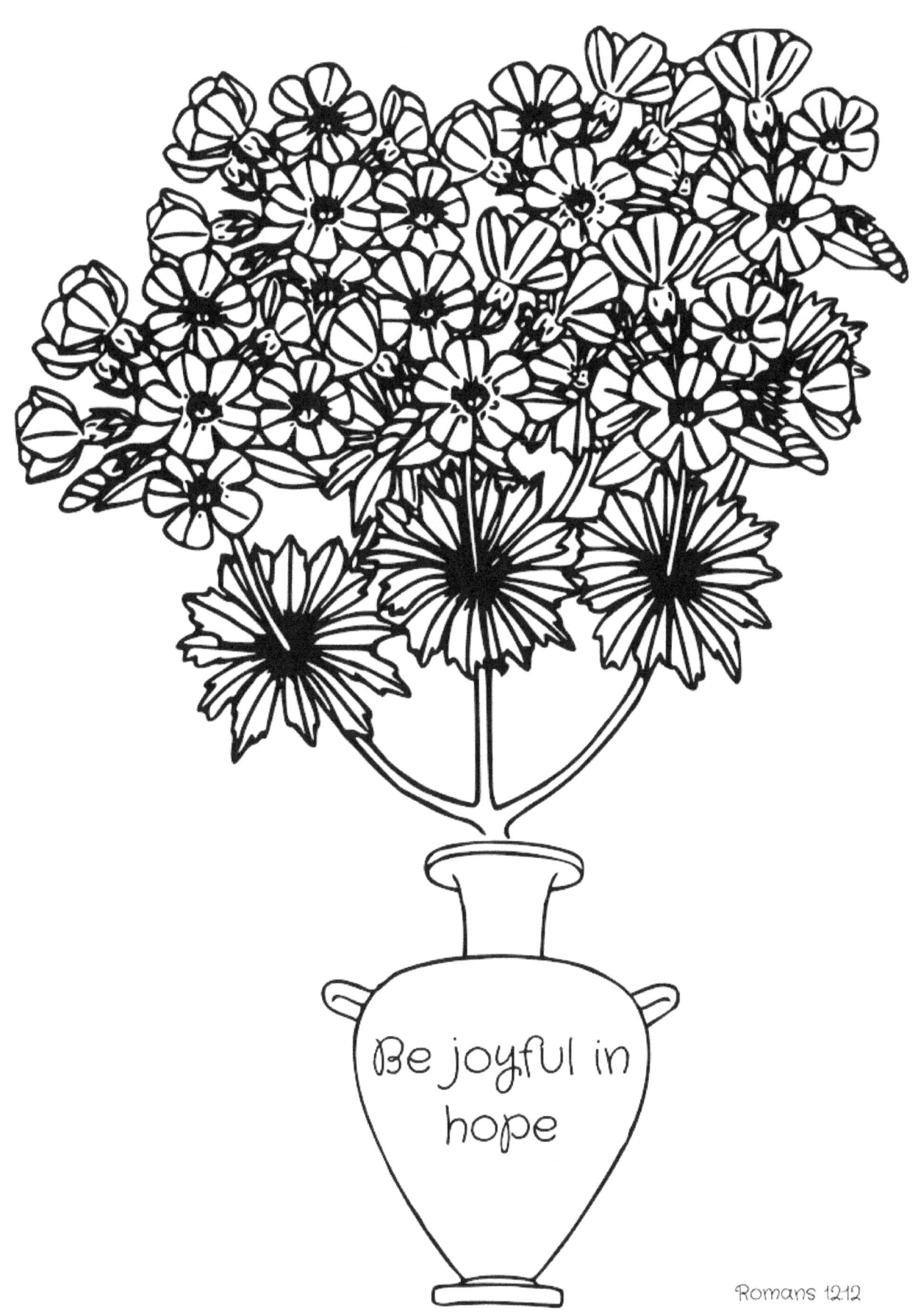

Be joyful in hope

Romans 12:12

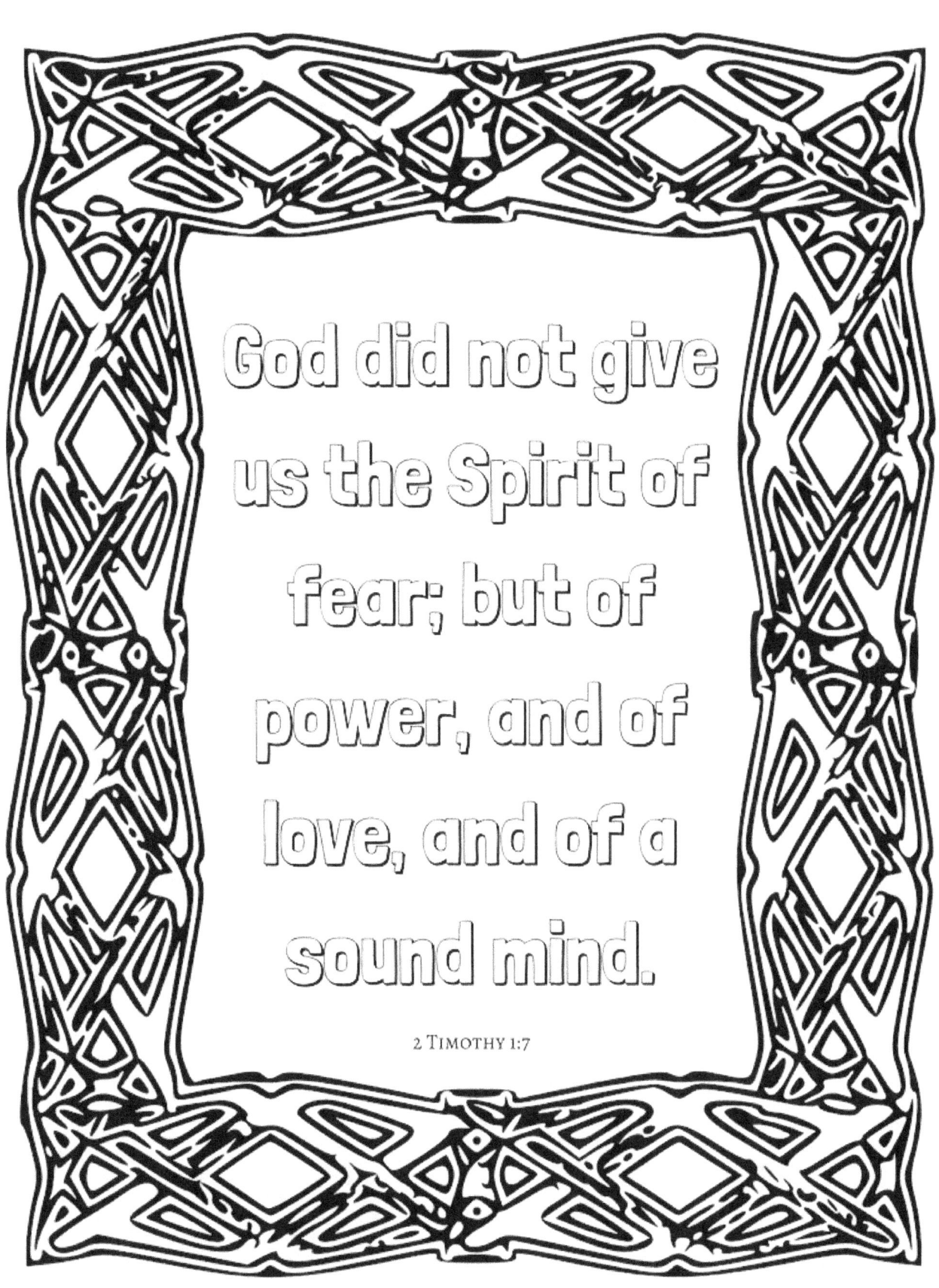

God did not give us the Spirit of fear; but of power, and of love, and of a sound mind.

2 TIMOTHY 1:7

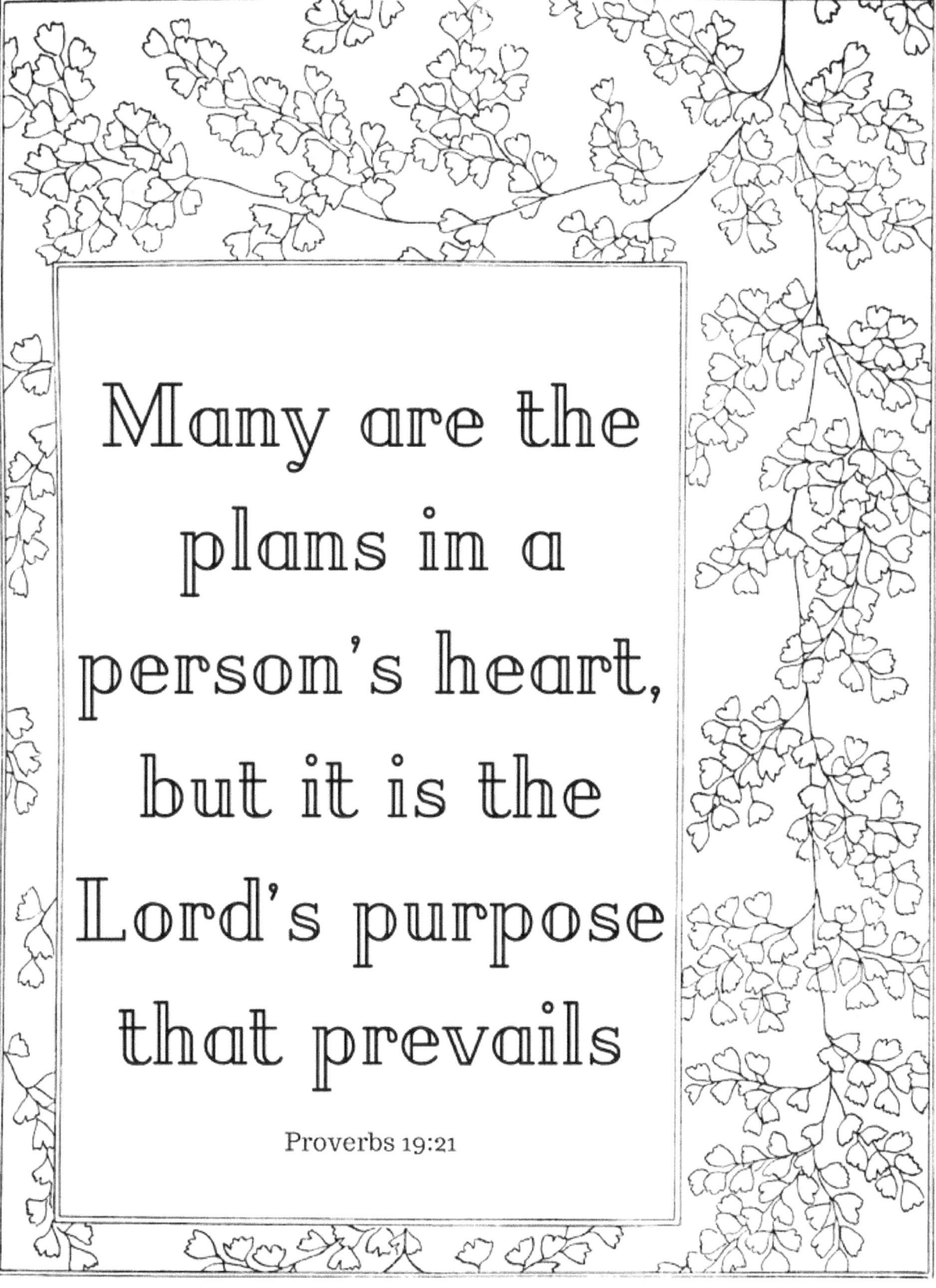

Many are the plans in a person's heart, but it is the Lord's purpose that prevails

Proverbs 19:21

Come to me,
all you who are weary
and burdened,
and I will give you
rest.

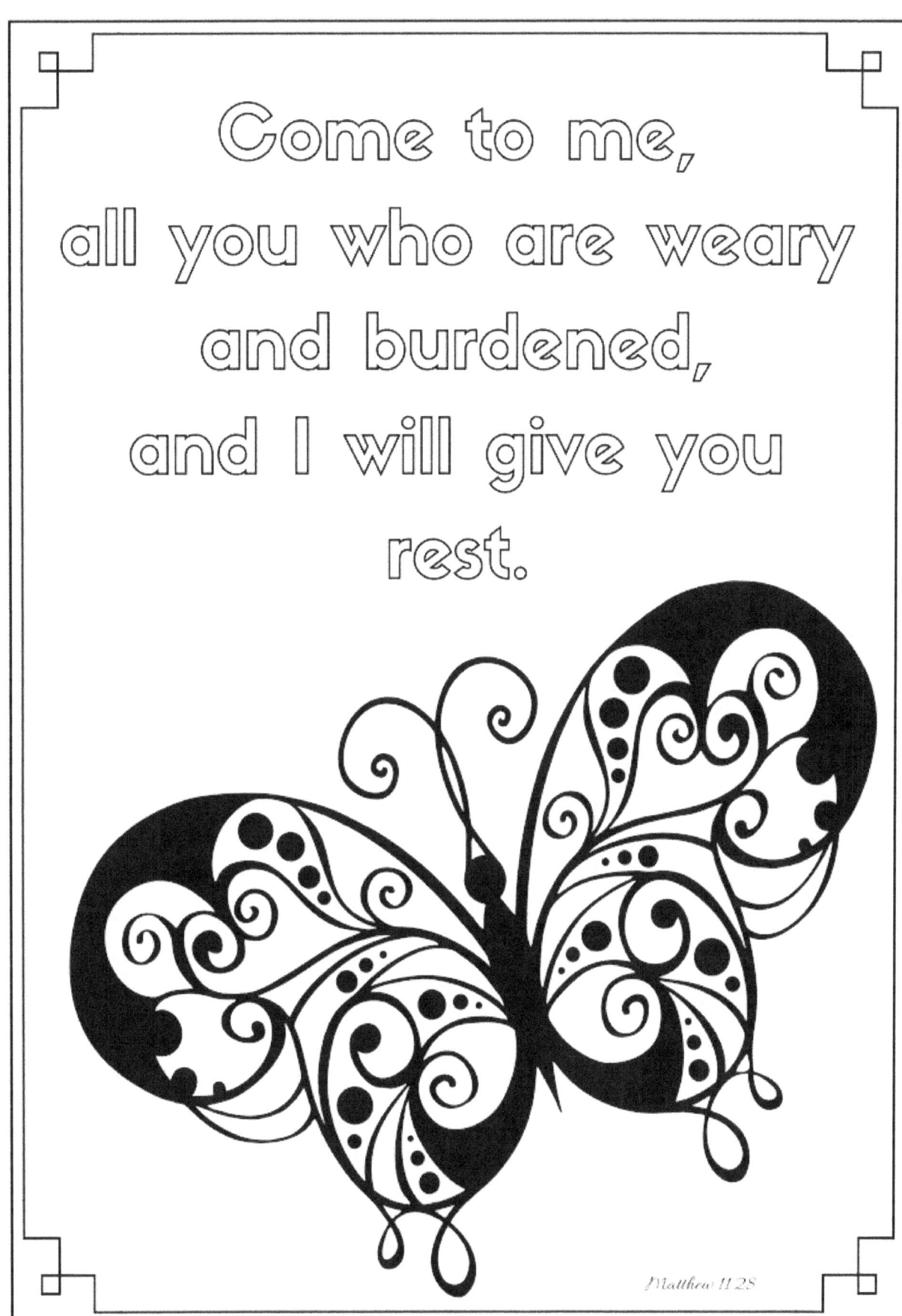

Matthew 11:28